Photography Backdrops

Creative and Inexpensive Ideas For Beginners and/or Amateur Photographers

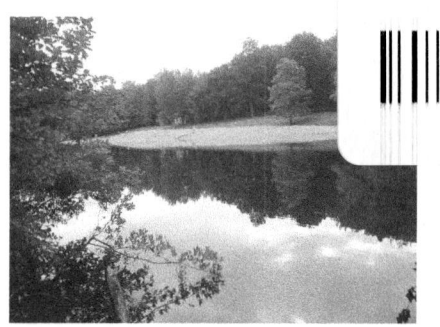

By: C Pazetti

ISBN-13: 978-1493660551

TABLE OF CONTENTS

Publishers Notes.. 5

Dedication... 6

Chapter 1- Created From Things Around The Home 8

    Curtains.. 8

    Rugs.. 10

    Shower Curtains... 11

    Old Bricks, Plaster or Peeling Paint... 12

    Balloons 17

Chapter 2- Choosing the Best and cheapest 21

Benefits of Choosing Natural Backdrops... 24

Chapter 3- Ideas for Any Photographer 26

Chapter 4- Inexpensive Backdrops and Props 34

Chapter 5- Vinyl Photography Backdrops 39

Create a Perfect Look... 41

    Create a Nostalgic Feel 42

Chapter 6- Using Natural Light 43

Chapter 7- Creative Resources.. 47

Chapter 8- Conclusion 51

Photography Backdrops

By C Pazetti

© Copyright 2013 C Pazetti

Reproduction or translation of any part of this work beyond that permitted by section 107 or 108 of the 1976 United States Copyright Act without permission of the copyright owner is unlawful. Requests for permission or further information should be addressed to the author.

This publication is designed to provide accurate and authoritative information in regard to the subject matter covered. It is sold the understanding that the publisher is not engaged in rendering legal, accounting, or other professional services. If legal advice or other expert assistance is required, the services of a competent professional person should be sought.

First Published, 2013

Printed in the United States of America

Book By The Same Author

PUBLISHERS NOTES

Disclaimer

This publication is intended to provide helpful and informative material. It is not intended to diagnose, treat, cure, or prevent any health problem or condition, nor is intended to replace the advice of a physician. No action should be taken solely on the contents of this book. Always consult your physician or qualified health-care professional on any matters regarding your health and before adopting any suggestions in this book or drawing inferences from it.

The author and publisher specifically disclaim all responsibility for any liability, loss or risk, personal or otherwise, which is incurred as a consequence, directly or indirectly, from the use or application of any contents of this book.

Any and all product names referenced within this book are the trademarks of their respective owners. None of these owners have sponsored, authorized, endorsed, or approved this book.

Always read all information provided by the manufacturers' product labels before using their products. The author and publisher are not responsible for claims made by manufacturers.

Paperback Edition

Manufactured in the United States of America

DEDICATION

This book is dedicated to all photographers that are interested in doing more with their camera and not just point and shoot most of all have fun, the more pics you take the more you will learn and develop your own persona.

Thank You For Buying This Book

People have come to appreciate the beauty of taking photographs. The idea of creating memories for years to come and for future generations is great and exciting.

However, gone are the days when photography was restricted to the studio with a black or white backdrop.

Photographers are allowing creativity in the world of photography hence making it better than ever before.

Cool, exciting and unique backdrops do not necessarily need to be expensive, the more creative the idea, the cheaper the backdrop.

Thanks to technology, you do not need to travel far and wide in search of inexpensive back drops, the internet has some brilliant ideas and accessible online stores for you.

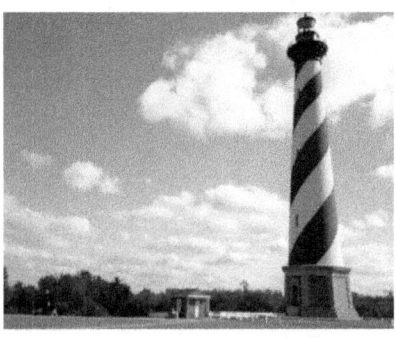

Chapter 1 - Created From Things Around The Home

Photography can be a rewarding, albeit expensive, vocation or hobby. Depending on one's budget and investment capabilities, the equipment can end up costing hundreds, if not thousands of dollars, but it does not have to. There are many ways in which one can cut back on monetary expenses and still take high quality photographs.

One of the easiest is one's choice in photography backdrops. There are many ways in which the professional or novice photographer can come up with beautiful and interesting backdrops by using items that are already on hand around one's home.

Curtains

Perhaps one of the most obvious backdrops can be created from one's own curtains. Curtains, of course, come in all kinds of textures, patterns and colors, so one's choices are virtually limitless.

It can be fun to layer various sheer curtains for different affects. The photographer can adjust his or her curtains in fun and interesting ways to control the light and to add visual interest.

They can be lit from behind with the natural light from the window, or the photographer can add simple floor lamps to light them from behind. In the latter case, care should be exercised not to allow the fabric from the curtains to come within direct contact with the curtain fabric.

Photography backdrops

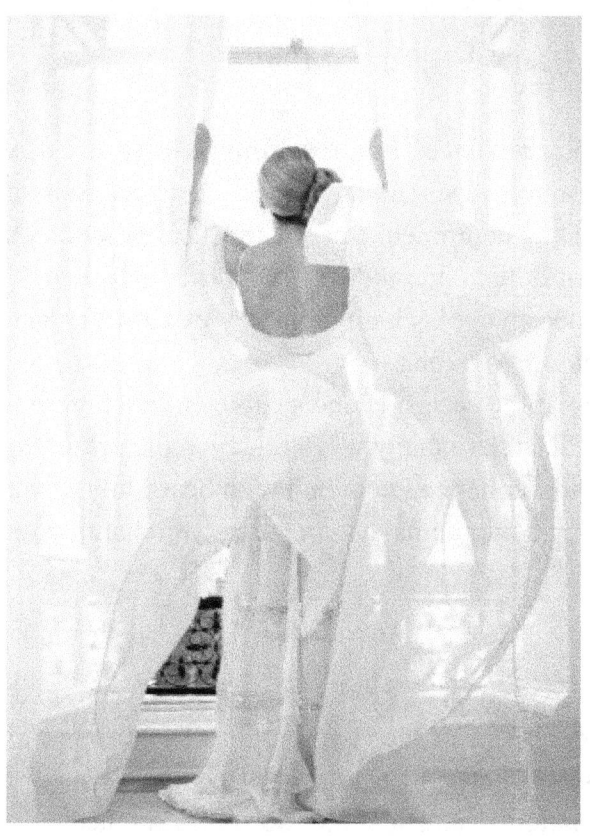

Rugs

Rugs, held horizontally by clamps on a curtain rod, can also make interesting backdrops. Whether one chooses the often rich, saturated colors from a contemporary abstract rug pattern or a vintage rug with subtle tones and design elements, the opaque quality of an interesting rug can help create a number of interesting looks

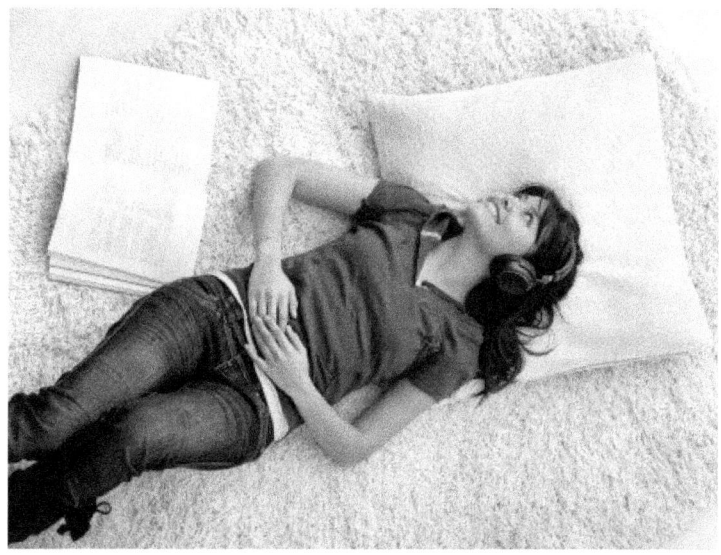

Photography backdrops

Shower Curtains

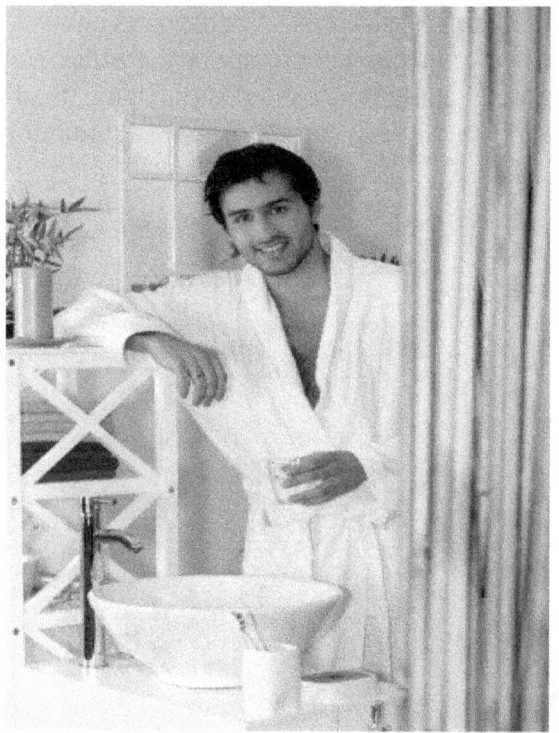

Shower curtains can be used in a number of interesting ways as backdrops for photography. They come in limitless numbers of colors and patterns.

The opaque ones can work well, of course, but getting creative with transparent or semi-transparent shower curtains can help create some stunning affects.

For instance a semi-transparent shower curtain with soft, low lights behind it can create a romantic ambience. Add colored lights behind a shower curtain for further interest
    Layer two clear, colored shower curtains, taking care to expose one color more than the other to add emphasis to specific tones.

Old Bricks, Plaster or Peeling Paint

Some may consider an old brick wall, peeling paint or outdated, heavy plaster finish eyesores, however, these elements can be amazing resources for the creative photographer.

Some of the most glamorous fashion photography shots have demonstrated the juxtaposition of elegant silks, furs and satins against the interesting and aging elements of bricks, plaster and peeling paint. Nothing works better to highlight the new and sophisticated than the inconsistent and opposite textures of these old walls and finishes.

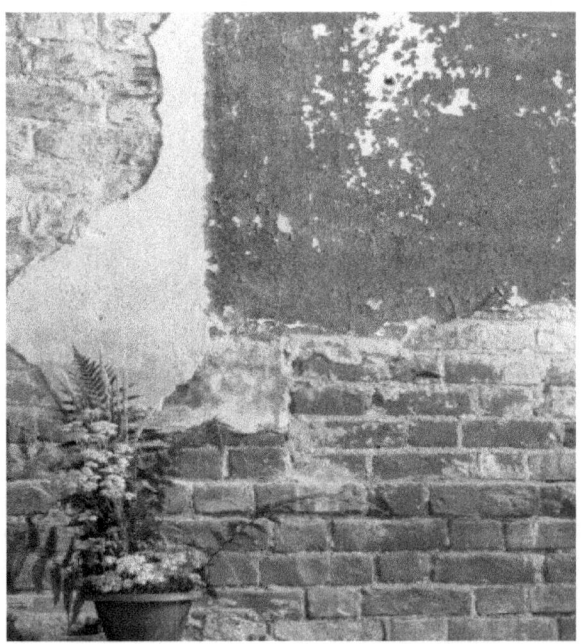

Pillows

One can create a specific mood by simply adding various pillows to a simple background, whether tossed on the floor, a chair or on a sofa.

Pillows are another option that comes in unlimited shapes, sizes, colors and textures. The photographer can add a single pillow for a slight pop of color or balance.

He or she can stack them at various heights to make towers of color or to draw the viewer's eye up or down, or they can be creatively used to create a mood of either serenity or chaos, depending on what the photographer wants.

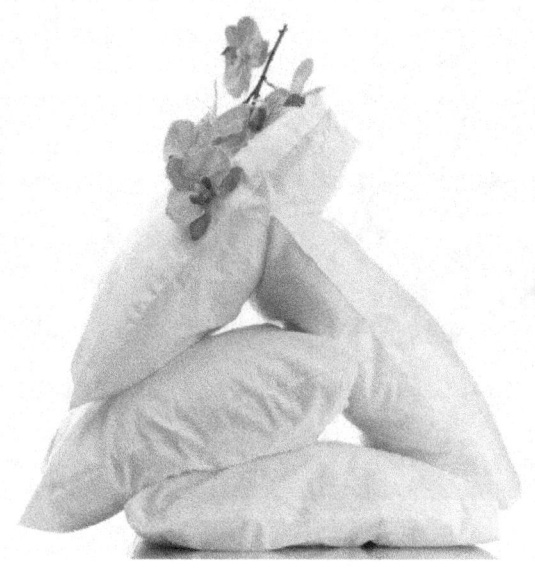

Cement

Josef Albers, the famous artist and color theorist, often talked about the effects that one color has on another, and how, when placed within close proximity to one another in certain amounts, one color can change how another color appears.

Placing a bright color in front of a plain, medium-toned, naturally colored cement wall can emphasize the bright color's vibrancy. When this technique is used with particularly bright or neon colors, the affect can be one of pulsating energy that seems to pop!

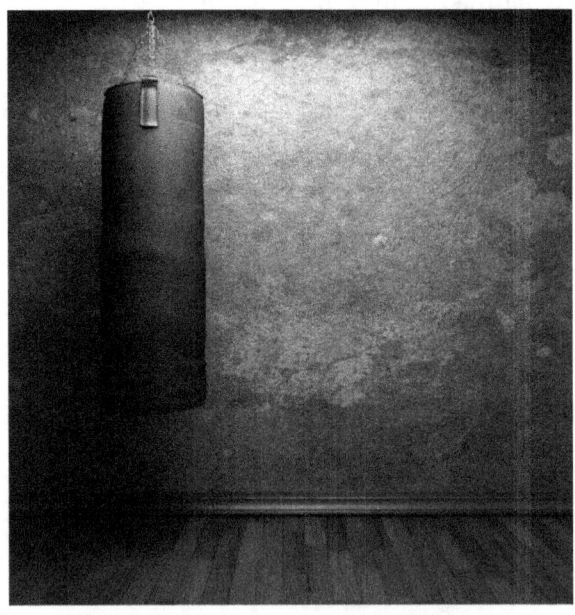

Cement can also be used in the same way as brick, plaster and peeling paint, to emphasis opposites and to make something new stand out against the mundane.

Cement gray has a way of absorbing light rays that make virtually any colored object look richer and more radiant.

Bed Sheets

Bed sheets can be fantastic backdrops for photography, both because of their versatile selections of appealing colors and patterns, but also because they can be hung in ways that either subdue or emphasize the light, depending on the photographer's intention.

They can be lit from behind or in front, for completely different looks, and can be pulled taunt or draped for even more photographic options.

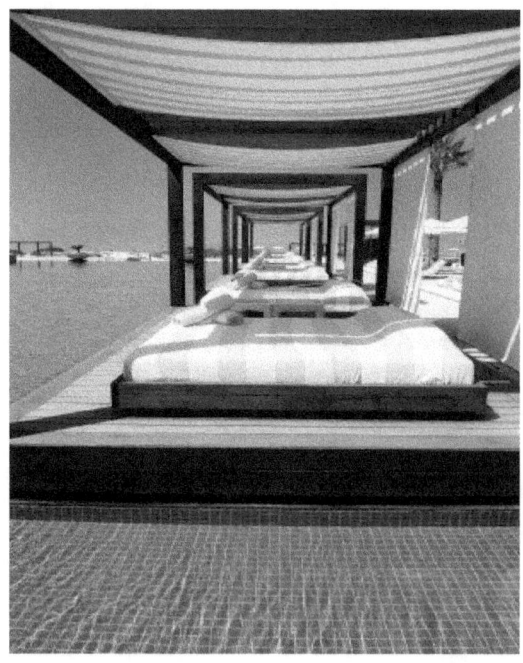

Balloons

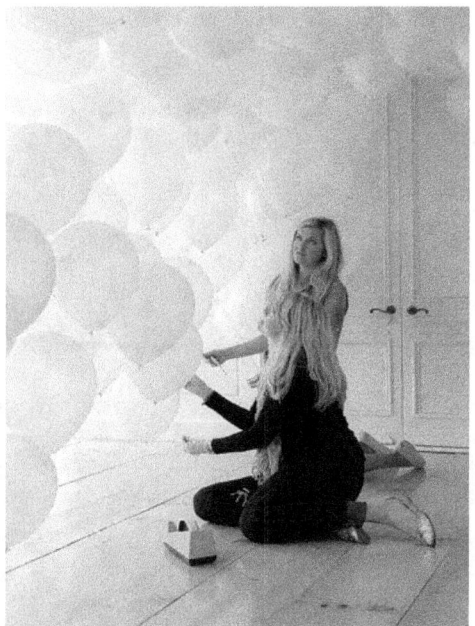

Angela Jacquin Photography

Reflections

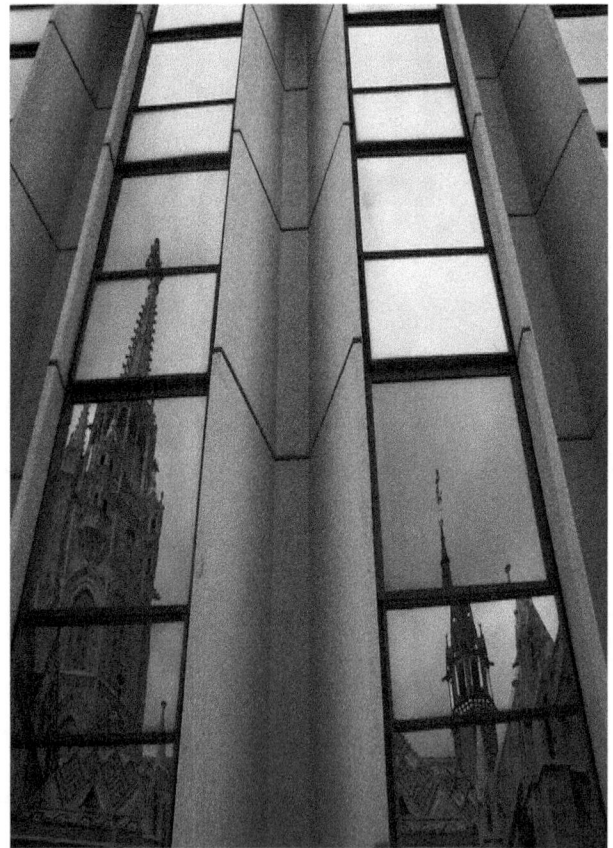

set up a tripod. shoot these photos using a slow shutter speed.

I like Rain

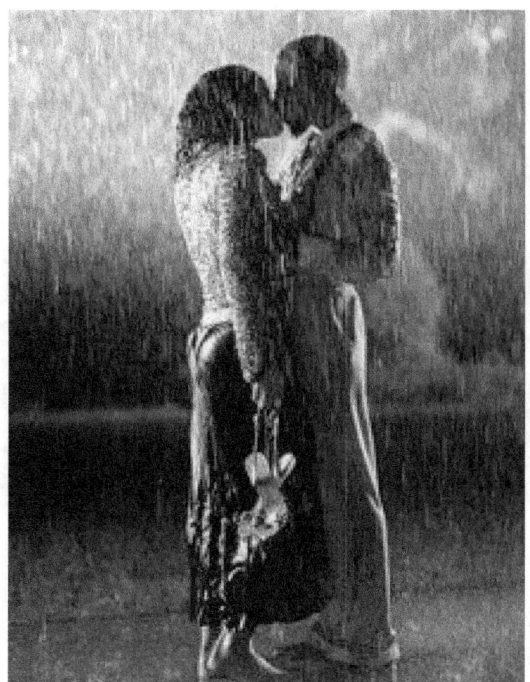

Brittany Stover Photography

Rain is a great prop. Make your camera water proof if not already, and a willing couple. Then set up a tripod. You will want to shoot these photos using a slow shutter speed so the rain drops will show. Take a few test shots once you have it down, the photos will be unforgettable.

Photography backdrops

Vibrant backdrop of South African Cape Town.

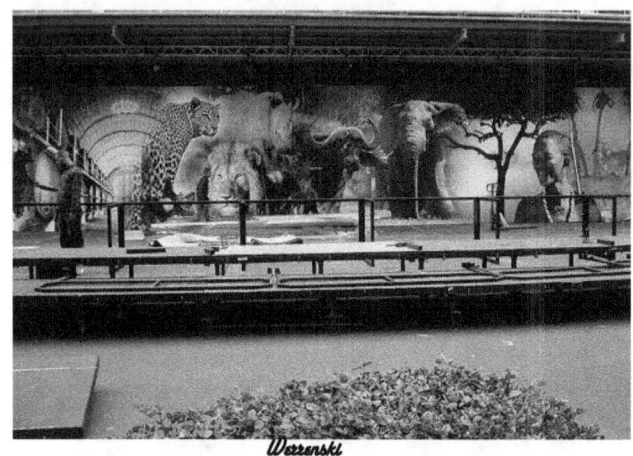

Chapter 2- Choosing the Best and Cheapest

After going through all the details of the camera settings and lighting effects the most common problem that new photographers face is choosing a backdrop. However it is not very difficult to choose a perfect backdrop which is completely free.

All you need is some knowledge and some creativity to apply that knowledge in the right way. Instead of spending huge amounts of money in creating backdrop for your portraits, you can use your surroundings as the backdrops for creating engaging portraits. most of the professional photographers also prefer natural settings for their backdrops as it gives them plenty of freedom.

Choosing the Right Backdrop

While choosing the backdrop you most choose a location that adds meanings to the photograph which you are taking. The backdrop should blend into the purpose of that photograph. Below are some ways you can find great backdrops:

Indoor Backdrops

There are several ways that you can use the indoor surroundings to spice-up your photographs. You can pose your subject at various places inside the house, but you should pay good attention to the proper lighting of that area.

For example, when posing your subject near a fireplace you should ensure that the fire is burning otherwise in the final print you would just see a black hole instead of a fire place.

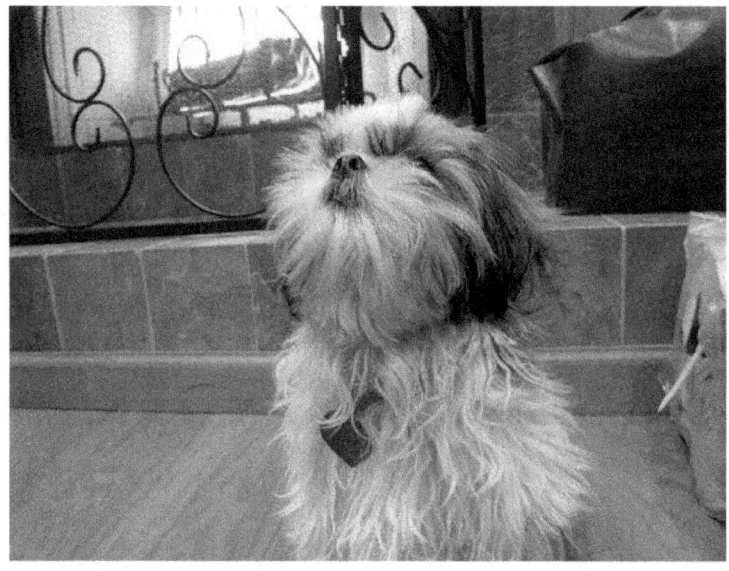

These precautions will help you in taking some really good photos. You can use the floor, the surroundings of the furniture, etc.

Outdoor Backdrops

Outside portraits are something that gives you many more options, but it's also true that this can create plenty of confusion among new photographers. You can use places from your backyard to beaches for making a good backdrop.

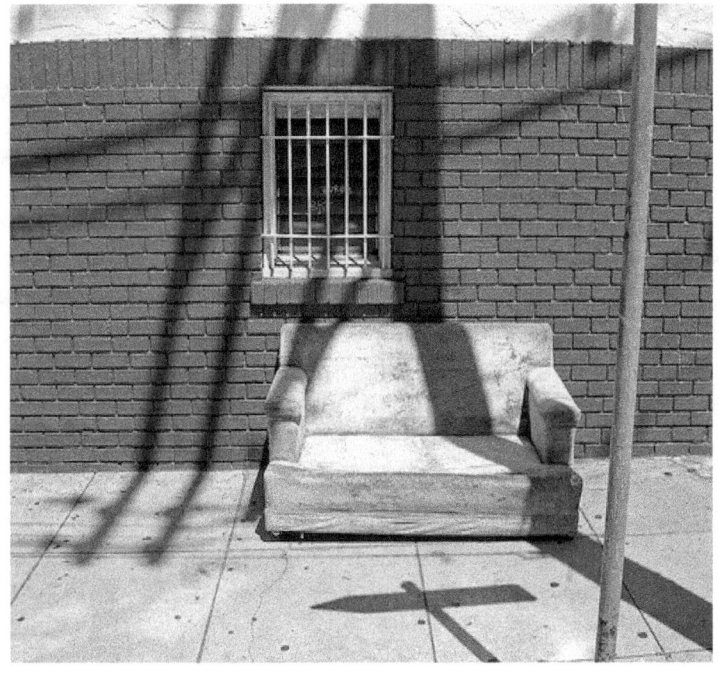

One of the most famous places is the local parks and they give very good options for beautiful backdrops. However it is important to take special care of proper lighting. You can also ask the subject if there is some place that they like which may have some meaning for them for that portrait.

BENEFITS OF CHOOSING NATURAL BACKDROPS

There are several benefits of using natural places as backdrops especially if you are a novice photographer. Some of these reasons are shared below.

Saves Money
You don't have to buy any expensive formal backdrops for creating portraits. Natural backdrops are cheap or inexpensive photography backdrops and can save you plenty of money which you can invest in other things like better camera equipment or add-ons.

Saves Time
Setting up a proper formal backdrop that is customized for the subject can take plenty of time. However using natural settings is about finding the right place and once you find it, then it doesn't take that much time for taking photographs.

Great Photographs
It is true that people relate to nature in a much better way. Therefore using nature as a backdrop in a proper way actually makes the photograph look much better than using some custom-built formal backdrop.

In Conclusion
If you are a novice photographer starting up in this field, you should remember that natural backdrops give you plenty of opportunity to explore the boundaries of photography.
Of course once you get comfortable with your equipment, you can invest in some backdrops, but don't forget that his best and inexpensive backdrops are all around you. In no time you will be seeing backdrops for your photo shoots everywhere.

Check the RESOURCE PAGE for more on backdrops

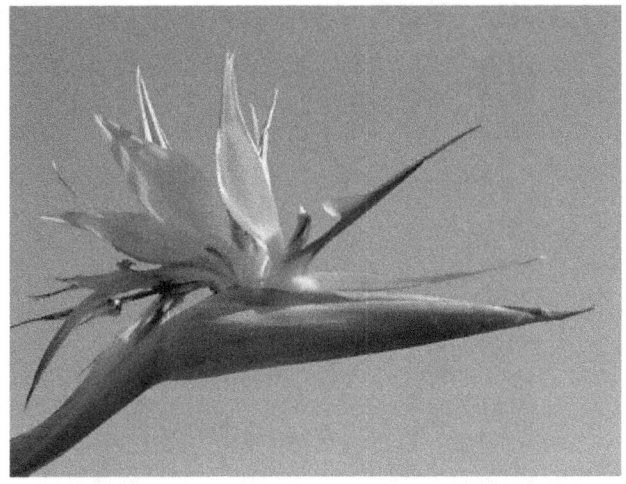

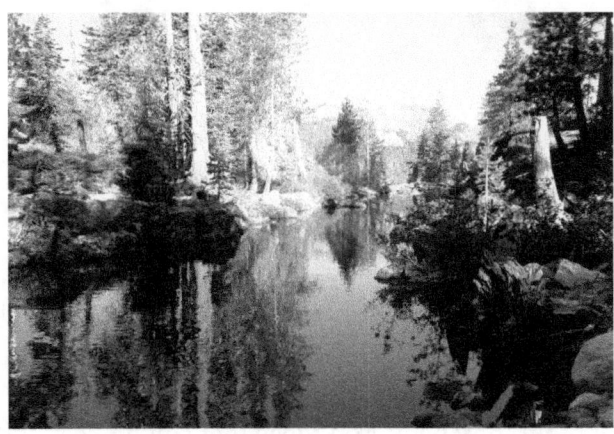

Chapter 3- Ideas for Any Photographer

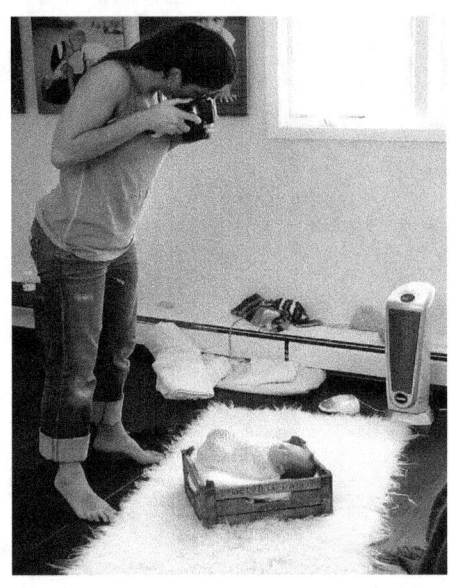

Photography backdrops play an important role in creating photos that stand out. You can focus the viewer's attention on a particular aspect of the photo just by using the right backdrop. A good backdrop serves many purposes.

It guides the viewer to focus on the main subject and helps accentuate the importance of the subject. Sometimes, the backdrop is used to complement the subject's appearance. There are many photography backdrop ideas that can be used with great effect to create stunning images.

This is the ultimate in photography backdrops. You can photograph a subject anywhere with any type of backdrop. After taking the photograph, just use an image editing software to select and remove the background, and then use any digital backdrop already available or newly created. While it is an easy. to do process, you need to pay attention to certain important things.

You most be adept in using the image editing software to make the photos believable. If at the time of photography, there was a light source behind the subject or if any colored reflected light was falling on the subject then you have to choose your digital background carefully.

If red light was reflecting on the subject and you choose a green backdrop then the difference will be noticed immediately and the photo will look contrived. You also need to take care of the perspective and match the background with the subject skillfully so that the photo does not look odd and out of place.

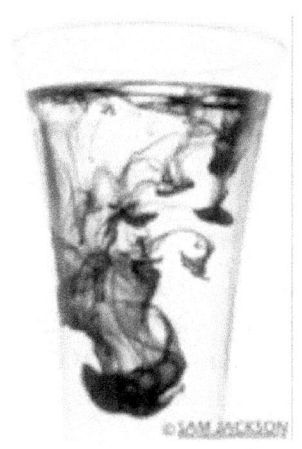

Fabric

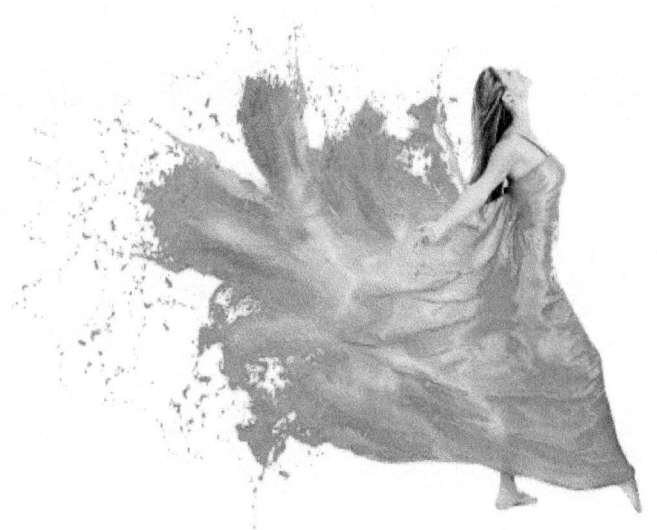

This is one of the simplest photography backdrops. The only thing you need to ensure is that the fabric length should be appropriate if you are photographing a person from head to toe. More the area you have to cover in the frame, longer and wider the length of fabric you will need.

The fabric should be long and wide enough so that the frame does not include background objects. Plain color fabrics can be used for most settings. If you do not have the required color of fabric then you have to buy it or paint an existing fabric in the desired color.

You also need to worry about the wrinkles and light transparency of the fabric. You can eliminate these problems by using an ironed fabric and using clips or pins to keep the fabric straight across all corners. Pin the fabric to a plain color wall so that there is no transparency problem.

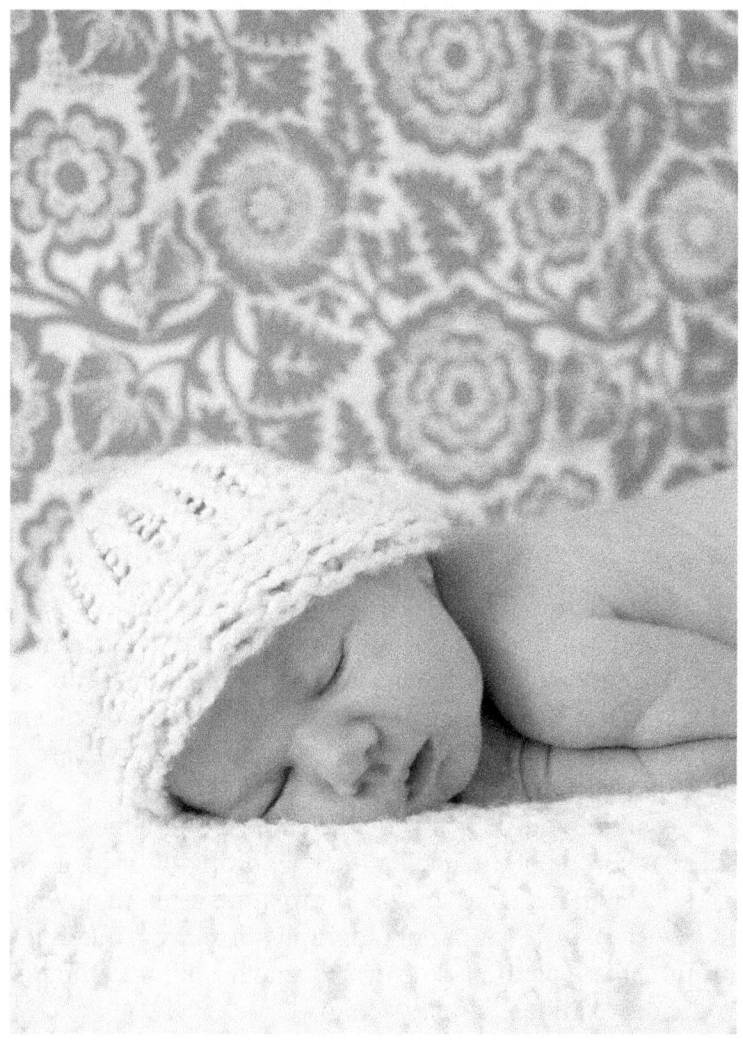

Paper

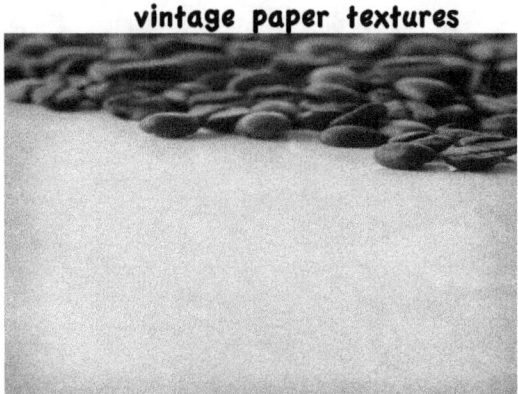

This is an excellent option to create photography backdrops. It is cheap and you can find papers in desired colors. You can attach small sized papers to each other to create a backdrop of desired width and length. You can even paint paper to create the desired effect. Paint in one color or create abstract images, there are unlimited possibilities here.

If possible, you should keep the subject a few feet away from the backdrop and then keep the backdrop out of focus in the photo. If you will be using the backdrop quite often then you should invest in professional photography backdrops like vinyl backdrops. This type of backdrops is standard in most studios and the product is available in many colors.

News paper is Not Just For Reading!

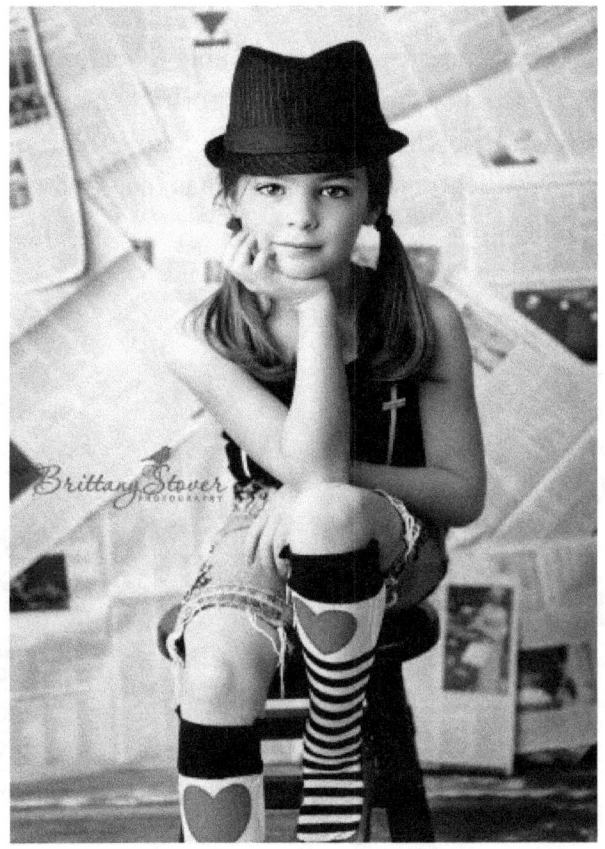

Chapter 4- Inexpensive Backdrops and Props

Backdrops and props are invaluable tools to a photographer, particularly when taking portrait shots, but prices can range from a few hundred bucks to a couple thousand. After emptying your wallet on a camera, who has that kind of money? No problem, there are cheap photography backdrops and props all around you.

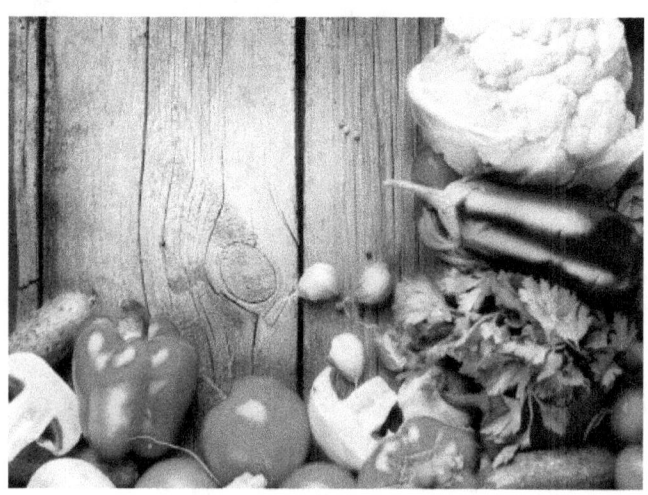

Nature's Calling

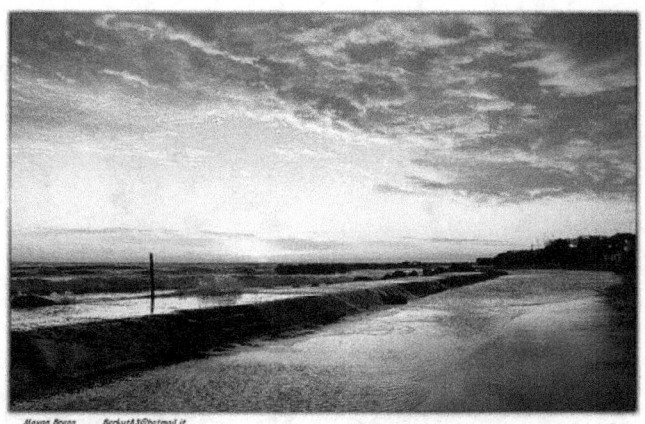

The purpose of a backdrop is to substitute for real life scenery. Why go for an obviously fake scene, when the real thing makes for so much better pictures? Get outside and visit the woods or a park.

Photography backdrops

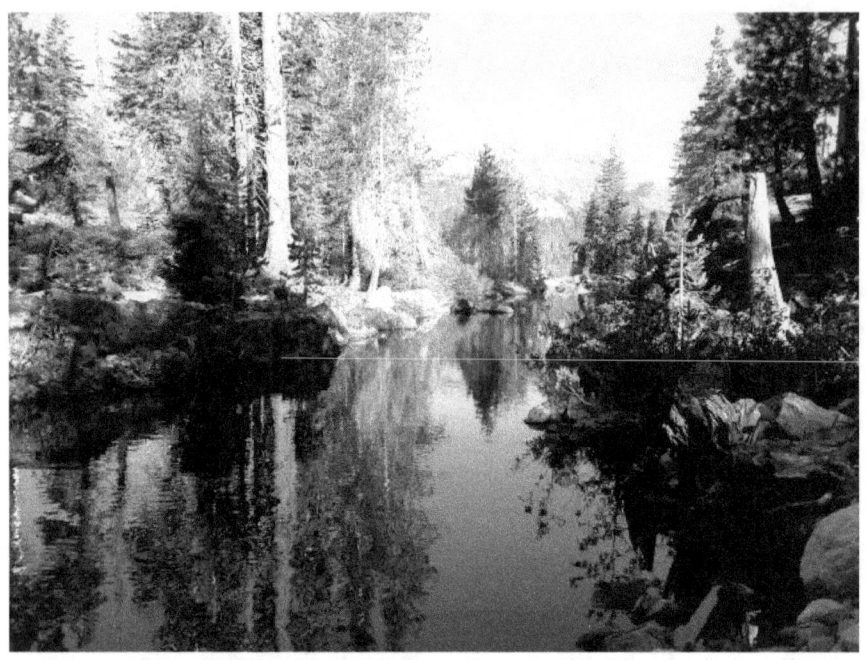

If you live in an area where nature is not easily accessible then head to a plant nursery.

The best thing about retail garden sections is that they are full of plants and garden decorations that you can rearrange into any position you want. Often times you will find that the sales people have already set up a nice scene to entice buyers into purchasing their products.

Let's Go Downtown

City escapes make great backgrounds. People love the rustic look of old buildings, and the grime of the street. It gives pictures an artistic urban feel that is often found in high end fashion photography.

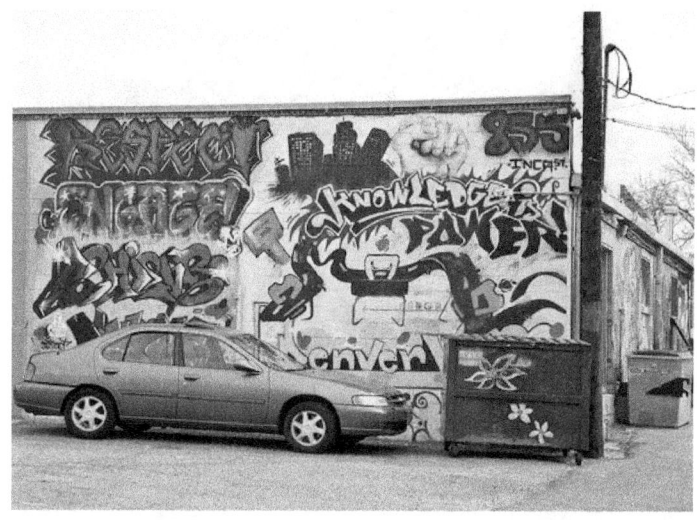

Of course you may not want to have uninvited guests in your pictures, avoid pissing off the locals, and head to the alley ways and back lots.

If the city is too far of a drive for you head to your local shopping center. The large sidewalls of retail buildings will give you a vintage city look. Go behind the store to where the trucks load and unload, get permission first though. Back there you will find all sorts of neat scene goodies like fire hydrants, chains, docks, and pallets.

What is the problem with reality? It never works the way you want it to. That is the other purpose of backdrops. Used indoors you can control the lighting to keep from having the picture look too dark or bright.

Well at least it was a problem back in the day when backdrops were invented. Today we have photo editing programs. Remember, when it comes to cheap photography backdrops and props, nothing beats the real thing.

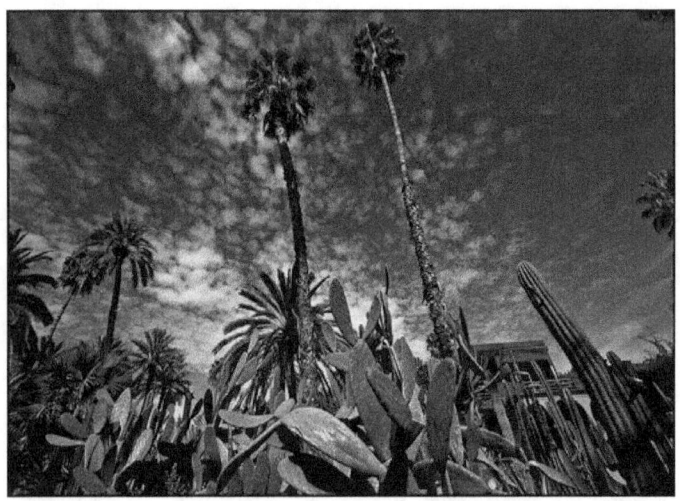

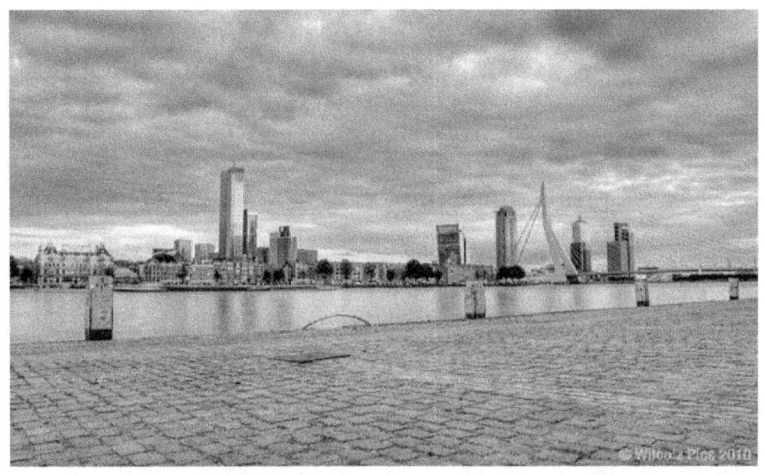

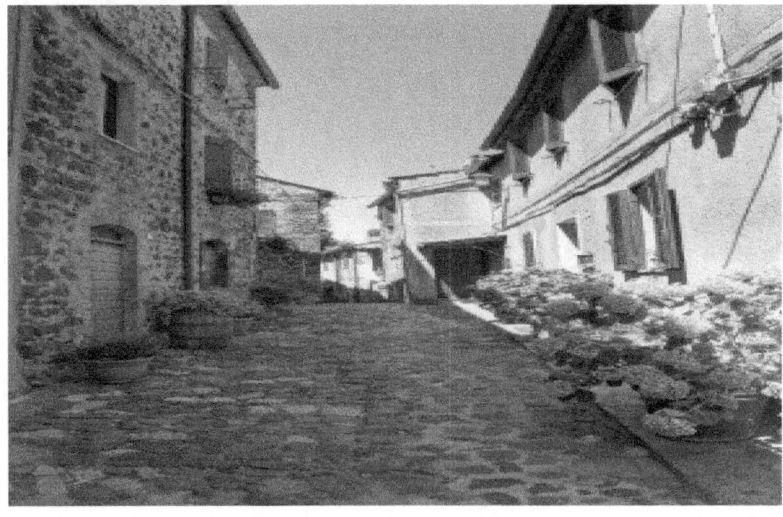

CHAPTER 5- VINYL PHOTOGRAPHY BACKDROPS

Photography backdrops are important in creating the right atmosphere for professional photographs. These backdrops are used for photographs in which you need to create special circumstances.

Vinyl photography backdrops are widely used these days due their several benefits. There are several types of vinyl backdrops that are available in the market some have glossy material or some have matte finish. Which one is the best for you depends on how and where you want to use them..

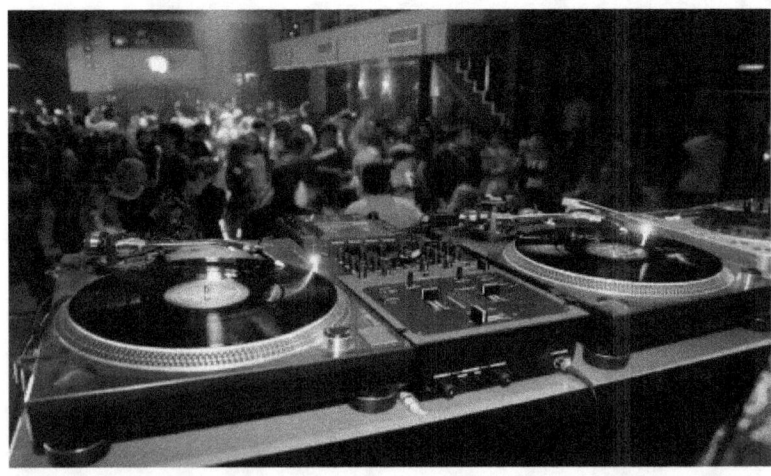

While using vinyl as backdrop you most consider some tips like do not take the backdrop to the floor unless you are doing full length photography. You most keep a distance of 5-6 feet between the subject and the backdrop or photos may show some wrinkles.

You can Write on It

You can use a vinyl backdrop that has some messages written over it which are relevant to the theme of the photo session. Let multiple people write the messages with pens of different color inks.

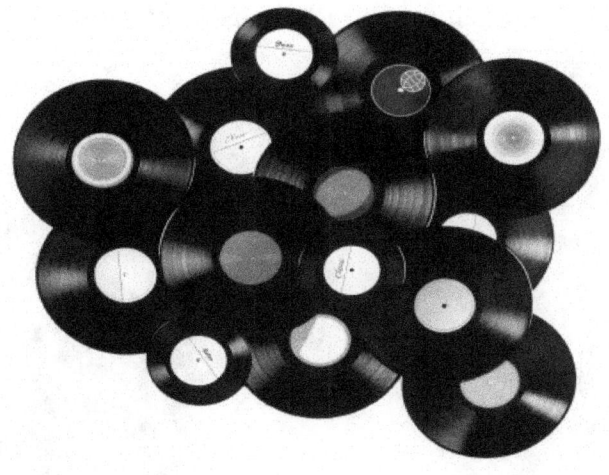

CREATE A PERFECT LOOK

Vinyl backdrops can be used as backdrops in wedding and several other functions. These backdrops create a perfect look that compliments the theme of the occasion. It is important to remember that for the occasion of parties you most go for a vinyl with a matte finish, as the glossy vinyl backdrops will give reflections of flashes in the photographs. Having vinyl backdrops is also a more economical option when compared to fabric or canvas backdrops.

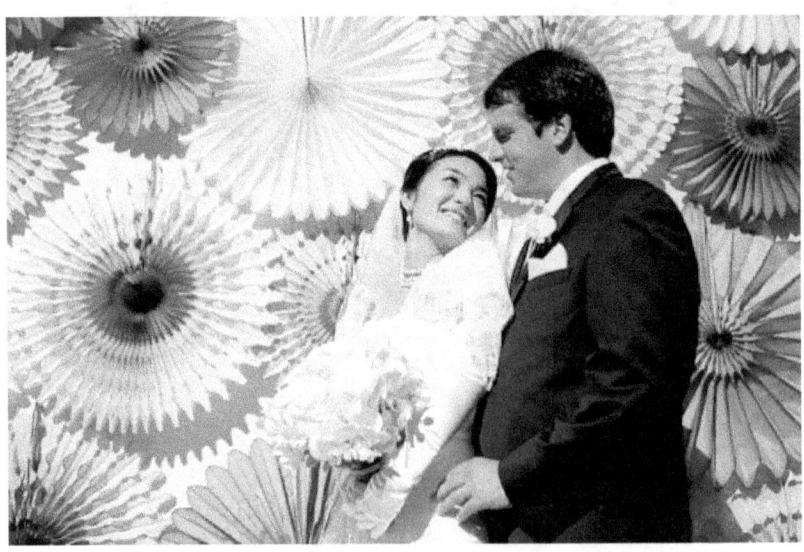

CREATE A NOSTALGIC FEEL

A good vinyl backdrop for family photo sessions would be to create a full length background using vinyl material. Then place ribbons of different colors at equal distances hanging vertically.

Keep the color of vinyl white and the ribbons can be red, pink, maroon, etc. Then along the ribbons hang the photos one below the other. Taking family photographs in front of this backdrop can create a nostalgic feel in the photos.

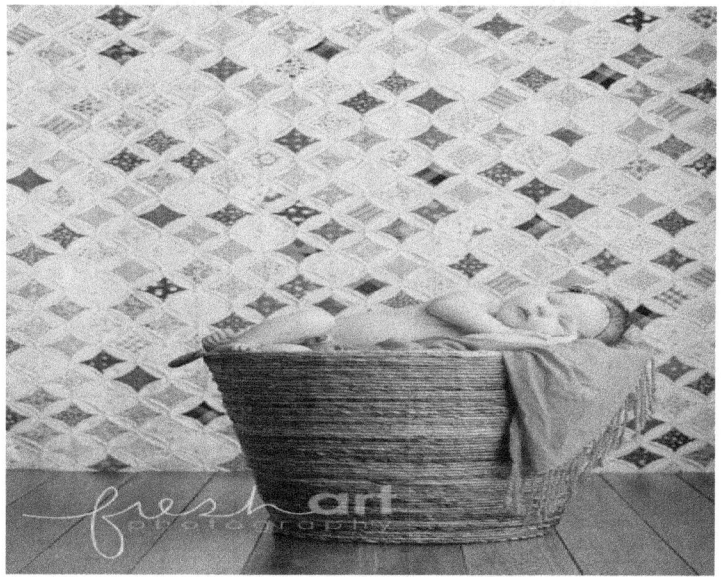

Chapter 6- Using Natural Light

Not everyone has to have expensive strobe lights to take good quality portraits. A great inexpensive way to get started doing photo shoots is to become a master at using natural light. Natural light photography does not mean just going outside and shooting in whatever light is available. It's about learning when the light is best and learning how to best manipulate the light to suit your purpose of taking great quality portraits.

Using this shot again as an example!

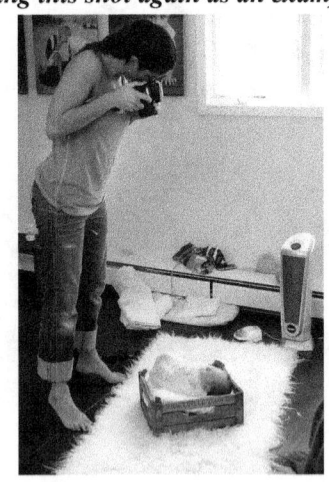

You can use natural light both indoors and outdoors. If you are indoors, you should place your subject at a 90-degree angle to a well-lit window, preferably north-facing. You can use a homemade reflector, such as a large white sheet or piece of poster board to help reflect some of the window light back onto the subject. Both the window and the reflector should provide some nice catchlights for the eyes.

Home made soft box

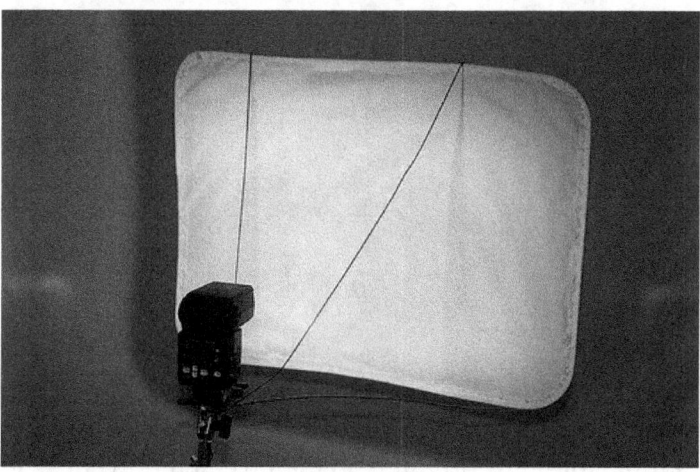

The best times of day to shoot outdoors are the hours right after dawn and right before dusk, with the hour before dusk being known as the "golden hour" because of the beautiful golden tone the sun provides late in the day.

By staying away from the mid-day sun, you will avoid harsh shadows and squinty eyes in your portraits. Squinty eyes in particular should be avoided at all cost, as a good portrait is all about the eyes. You can help prevent squinting by using even shade outdoors wherever possible.

Reflectors can be used outdoors as well, both with your subject in the shade and when they are backlit. Backlighting is to put the light source, in this case, the sun, behind your subject. It can create a beautiful glow on the back of the subject, and it also prevents squinting because there is no uncomfortable light shining in the subject's eyes.

Home studio materials: vinyl, foil, umbrella spot lights

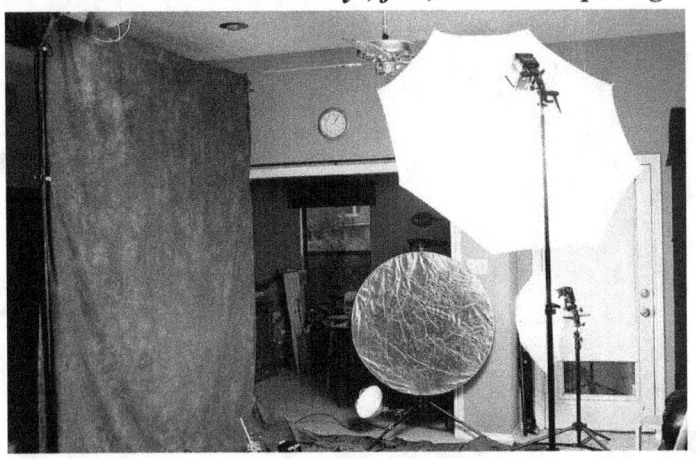

Using a reflector helps brighten up the face and prevent shadows. There are inexpensive commercial reflectors available, but the previously mentioned white poster board works just as well, as does a large picture frame covered in aluminum foil. Make sure that if you are experimenting with backlighting that you use a lens hood, or something to shade the lens to help avoid lens flare in your pictures.

When using natural light photography, it is a good idea to shoot in RAW mode, with your white balance set to Auto. Even when doing your best to control the lighting, there can be a lot of variables that change rapidly when you are using natural light.

By shooting in RAW mode, you have the flexibility to adjust the white balance and exposure to the photographs easily during your RAW conversion to jpeg images.

Chapter 7- Creative Resources

Book by the Same Author
selling your Photos online.

It only takes a creative mind to come up with a perfect photography background. A great background contributes to the quality and appeal of the photo so shopping for some cheap backdrops online is a great idea.

Kids

most parent prefer that their children take photos every now and then so as to mark their milestone. These little people are fun and therefore demand a fun backdrop that brings out their personality but remains unique at the same time.

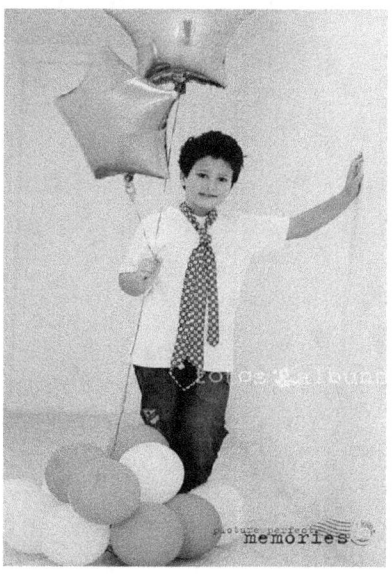

The cheapest way that you could do this is by blowing up some balloons and pinning them on a plain cardboard. The balloons can be of different colors and sizes to add variety. This is a very unique idea that is bound to make any kid's picture fun and lively.

For a young boy's photo shoot, you could definitely go for a bed sheet with his favorite cartoon character. Ensure that the corners are tightly pinned so as to produce a flat surface.

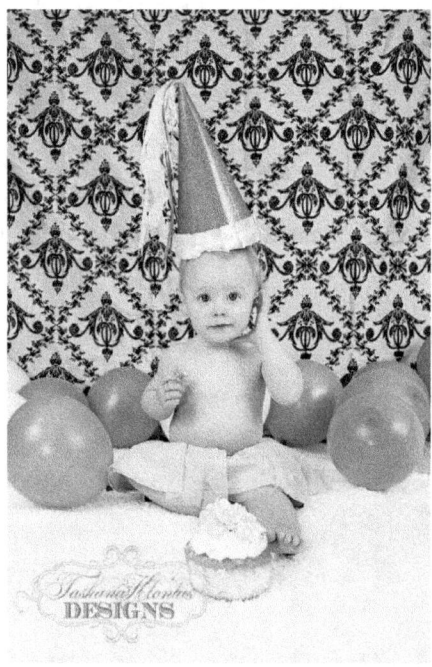

The same case applies for a girl with princess themed bed sheets. This kind of backdrop can be purchased from, *creative studio backdrop ideas for photograph*

Ladies

Women are known to like flashy things that make them seem important and relevant in the society and the work place at large. In this case, it would take a little creativity to make them feel like the celebrities that they really are.

When you think of a diva, classy shoes, expensive clothes and jewelry come to mind. In this case, you could try getting a white piece of clothe and a red one to step on signifying the red carpet. Have her all gleamed up and looking like a superstar.

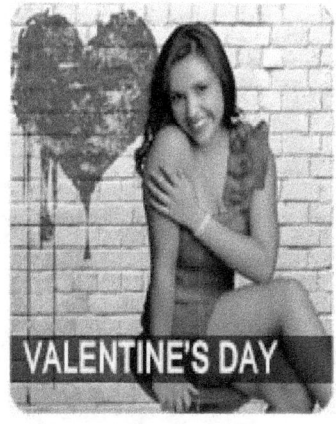

On the other hand, if you really want to go all out, nature might come in handy. Set up in a cool, green and shady place, tie a bunch of high heeled shoes each on its own and have them hang from the tree at different lengths.

This setting is unique, definitely brings out the diva in her and eventually produces a perfect photograph. This and similar ideas could be seen at, *Backdropoutlet.com*

Men

Men are known to be relaxed and live a very simple and relaxed life. They are not to complicated or strict when it comes to photographs but this doesn't mean that they do not like the good things in life. In their case, you could choose to go for a simple wood block for their back ground.

This could be a continuous ply of wood or several pieces stuck together with a nice finishing. This idea is creative, unique and definitely cost effective. To make the search easier, you could turn around the wardrobe in the bedroom or the book shelf.

A muslin cloth fabric could also be a great idea for this. To see these ideas and styles at Muslinscheap.com, has the perfect solution for you.

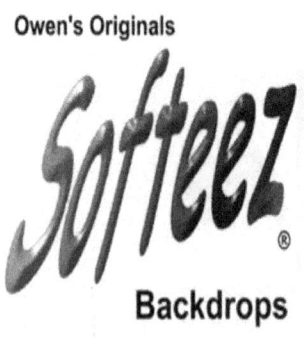

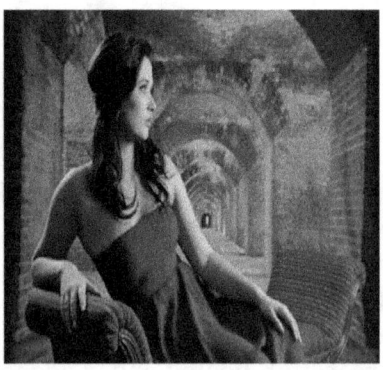

A few more other places that you could buy cheap backdrops online include:

dgrin.com, dhgate wholesale, drop it modern, Amazon

CHAPTER 8- CONCLUSION

Vinyl photography backdrops are famous because they are durable and economical to use and used in a right way, they can bring creative uniqueness in your photographs.

A Pic with a Perfect Backdrop Says A 1000 Words.

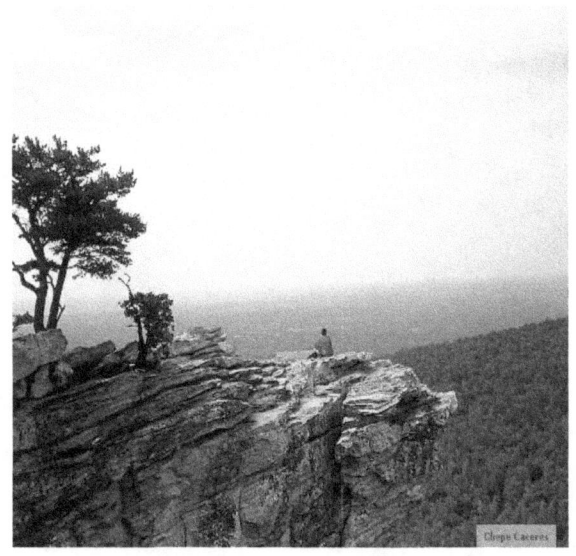

www.ingramcontent.com/pod-product-compliance
Lightning Source LLC
Chambersburg PA
CBHW071827170526
45167CB00003B/1449